THE HIGHWAY OF LIFE

and

A Collection of Earlier Writings

Best wishes,
Virginia Hult

By

Virginia Hult

FOREWORD

Our grandma has always been a writer. We each can remember reading the different chapters of *A Poodle's Tale*, about life from the perspective of Grandma's little dog, Pepper. The stories always put smiles on our faces.

In the spring of 2015, we each had a chance to talk to Grandma and asked her to do some more writing. The next thing we heard was: Grandma is writing a story called *The Highway of Life*. We are both really looking forward to reading Grandma's book about her perspective and philosophy of life as well as reading the other pieces she has written.

Grandma, we want to tell you how much we have enjoyed and appreciated the late night talks, the phone conversations, all of the family reunion card games, the personally knitted hats and scarfs, the piano lessons, and the pieces of advice you have shared with each of us over the years.

We love you very much, Grandma, and want to thank you for everything you do and for who you are.

Love,
Dana and Kyle

INTRODUCTION

What began as a simple piece of writing in answer to an inquiry has snowballed into a creation of wonder. How, I wonder, do my meandering thoughts become a book?

When my grandson, Kyle, asked me if I had done any more writings and my granddaughter, Dana, asked if I would put some thoughts about life in writing for her, what grandmother could refuse them? A grandchild wants to hear what their grandmother has to say! Surprise, surprise. I hope I don't disappoint them.

Many thanks to Pastor Michael O'Brien, visiting chaplain, who happened to drop in to visit and expressed an interest in reading the few paragraphs that I had written in response to their requests. He strongly suggested that it be published. He had had a pleasant experience of self-publishing with an Amazon affiliate. I immediately refused to consider that. With his persuasive ways, he pointed out how much the grandchildren would enjoy seeing the material in print, thus selling me on the idea.

Pastor Mike was instrumental in guiding us through the maze of stages associated with self-publishing. If I hadn't been in home hospice, I might never have met him. What a loss that would have been!

Thanks most of all to my daughter, Lisa. She worked many late night hours handling all the requirements and using unknown computer skills to bring this to fruition, completely due to her nature of never giving up on a job once it is started.

V. Hult - April 2015

Table of Contents

A Poodle's Tale

A dog with an attitude speaks her mind.

The Highway of Life

is dedicated to Dana and Kyle

who motivated me

to put some thoughts on paper.

THE HIGHWAY OF LIFE

Life is like a trip on a long highway. Hopefully, you have a long trip. You will get on the road or highway and proceed forward. It is always forward, well, maybe some short jogs sideways. The road will be bumpy sometimes, up or down, curvy and straight. There will be beautiful views, wide vistas, new experiences and sights for you to experience and see. Doesn't that sound a lot like life? There will be rough roads sometimes, even dangerous conditions. The weather won't always be pretty. Some stormy weather you are bound to run into. The longer your trip on this highway of life the more experiences you will have.

There will be many other people on this highway with you. People all around you. Some nice people, some not so nice. They may be making a quicker trip than you and might speed past you. They can also slow you down. You have to adjust your speed to accommodate the conditions. You won't be able to drive on this highway until you're legally old enough. There are rules and laws that you have to obey and understand. You will most likely depend on your parents or friends at that time to guide you.

Now, once your parents are no longer responsible for you, you must take over the wheel. Whoa, this is big! Well, you've been waiting, it seems, for a long time. When society considers you legally able to maneuver on their highways, to know and respect the rules, you will be responsible for the choices you make. Your choices affect other people, you know. A society needs people who make good choices, choices that cause harm to no one. A life with respect for yourself, for all living beings and things, will give you a glorious life as you travel the highway of life.

There will be scary stretches and accidents on this highway. Conditions can be catastrophic! There might be wrecks strewn all over the road. Do you make it around them? Maybe, maybe not. You make adjustments and might need some repairs or replacements. You may even change your plans for the trip. The idea is to keep going. Always forward. Living life is like traveling on the highway of life; exciting, challenging, rewarding, surprising.

Open Road Transit Specialized Services, that's me. Or rather a side line that I have. Just call me Mattie. I contract with Triangle Trucking Company out of Kansas City to handle less-than-full-truck load shipping for them on occasion. LTFT trucking. It's an ideal job for me. I like to get out of the house once in awhile. Sometimes even more. I love the freedom of travel, the new experiences, and all the different sights to see. What better canvas than the map of the United States of

America to cover! Can you ask for more variety than that? I started the business before I was married so Mac didn't expect me to give it up when he came along. It's my open door, an escape valve, a nice excuse to do what I like when the feeling hits me.

I'm a trucker, a part time lady trucker. Don't ask me my age or my weight and we'll get along just fine. You may ask: What does it take to be a good trucker, on this highway of life? That's a legitimate question.

Trucking on today's highways takes concentration, awareness, attention to detail, eye-hand coordination, and good peripheral vision to know what's in front of you, beside you, behind you. You need patience and endurance for tension during traffic. How long can you sit in a traffic jam, remain enclosed, confined, packed in with crowds of occupied vehicles? You might spend hours with hundreds of victims stranded on some divided bridge. You may have to. If you did, would you throw a fit? Scream and rage at fate? Some individuals would show signs of juvenile tactics with temper tantrums and uncontrolled rage, with fruitless attempts to relieve the situation. They might be helpless with no physical remedy available to them. They should find a more sedentary life.

Do you have the wisdom to say to yourself "I can't change the situation so I better make the best of it."? Think, "What would I do at home if I were locked in my room for an hour? Wow, great. I'll go back to bed and

3

sleep, thank you very much." Or, "I need to make a shopping list for that next school project." Time is valuable, time is the one thing we can decide how we spend. Time is the ONLY thing that is ours alone. Spend it wisely and be rich in spirit.

I deliver things that make people happy, comfortable, enriched, important items needed by individuals and businesses. I travel all over the U.S., in good weather and bad, on roads that can be good or bad. There are quiet, steady times, boring delays, traffic pile-ups. But the beauties! The sights! Have you ever taken the time to enjoy a SUNRISE or a SUNSET? If you haven't, be sure you do. Mountains, rivers, miles of prairie, what variety! Fields of grain! Sunflowers in a field all facing the same direction. Cattle standing together, no place to go. What an education you will get when you take a trip around this country.

The other day I was remembering a trip I made when I was first starting out. I had a delivery to make, a load of tires from Akron, Ohio, to Detroit. I knew the traffic would be heavy in such congested areas. I was nervous as hell. What would happen if I were late? I was hoping the roads would be good and clear. It was January. The roads were not good or clear. Just on the outskirt of town I started to slide sidewise, I had no control. Oh Boy! Where will I end up? Sweet Jesus!!! This load is shifting. Whoa... I'm going to crash. Cars are sliding every which way. I'm going to die! And I just got started, -- ah ---- Hold on now. The tires are starting to grab, they're getting traction again. Slow down now, slow, slower. Phew... Calm down, the worst is over. My heart is thumping like crazy. Take a deep breath. No, take a few. That was a close call. Yes, I'll be a little late making this delivery, but better late than never.

I was privileged to deliver very expensive things that needed special handling, such as: some with delivery time specificity, a rush job, or difficult location access. Dead-heading might be involved, that is heading to one location and bypassing other stops along the way. Joe Carlson of Triangle Trucking would call me for some of these special deliveries. Just often enough for me to keep my place in the business. The money was good.

I transported a beautiful A.B.Chase grand piano, such a fine piece of furniture, and I'm sure the tone was out of this world. I delivered it to the Cleveland, Ohio Symphony Orchestra and I got to wondering who will be playing it. I'd have loved to hear it. Probably some young genius will turn it into a rippling, smashing, thrilling masterworks. How much practice does it take to accomplish works like that? Hours at a stretch, days at a time, months, years. It's practice, practice, practice. Repetition over and over. Endlessly repeating the works. When does muscle memory kick in? What a thrill, a relief, when that takes over for stretches at a time. Now, a tricky part will be coming up...keep your place. OH...A GOOD SAVE. This must be a God-given talent, maybe an inherited gene, like your eye color.

Well, I've been rambling on, been driving all this time. Or did you know that? My exit is coming up. I need a cup of coffee. This truck stop is known for its pies. I am going to make a stop after this break at the upcoming weighing station, get my hours recorded, get checked out. How I used to hate all those regulations when I was young. Now, thank goodness for them. They keep me safer and everyone else on the highway. There are so many more vehicles on the road than when I started, streams of cars, like rivers of lemmings racing to get there, where ever that is.

Well, I'm back on the road, picking up the trip where I left off. A nice steady go, it should be a good day. There are a bunch of big rigs out front. Those big six wheeler and sixteen wheelers are masters of the road, rolling ahead with such authority. Their size is impressive. Yes, size matters in some things.

Being in the flow of traffic on this highway of life is a most personal experience. As various as the views, traveling gives you a wealth of experiences, which is a part of your education. There is no substitute for actual participation in an experiment. Seeing is believing. No one can tell you about a subject that will have as strong an impact on you as actual involvement. If you are curious by nature you will naturally enjoy and benefit from the experiences of traveling that much more.

There is such beauty! Such freedom! The joy of traveling with the road rolling ahead of you gives you time to think: reminisce, stroll through memories. where else can you have time to daydream, make plans, and consider options?

My rig gives me so much satisfaction with all the comforts of home: air conditioned, heated seats, phone, and music at my fingertips. I can curl up in the back with my down comforter, call it a day when I feel like it. What's not to like? Sure, I name my rigs, they are my partners. This one's Charley. They have been loyal, faithful, some better built and more dependable.

Occasionally, I'll hire on a helper but I prefer to work alone. During school breaks, my kids take turns accompanying me on some deliveries. They love it and it adds to their education in many ways.

Traveling life's highway is, to me, equivalent to our moving along our life's path traveling forward in time over the bumps in the road and thrilling at the beauty, the wonder of it all! Sometimes by ourselves, or in intimate circles, we move in our chosen group. This is LIFE. This is LIVING. The blessings abound. Forward, always forward. Our destination ahead is unknown to us! We'll know it when we get there, but not before. What a thrill, a surprise.

A new day dawning! Sunrise!!! Looking out your window is not experiencing a SUNRISE. You've got to be in it, with the bare sky above you. Feel the temperature of the air, the moisture on your skin. Notice the quiet, no sound. Well, maybe some crickets. Use all of your senses. I feel possessive of mornings. Mine, mine, mine. Is this all for me? Well, why not? We don't have to tell anyone. Anyway, there's enough for everyone.

What a gorgeous time of day! This is the day which the Lord has made. I will rejoice and be glad in it. I am euphoric. If the weather is perfect the euphoria lasts even longer. Everything is starting over again, fresh, clean. A new beginning. Driving is at its best in the morning, smooth, fast. The natives are not out so traffic will be light. Driving feels so good. Places look their best even coated with a film of moisture. I have the road to myself.

This up-coming trip will be one of those long ones. I'll be away from home for some stretch. The family will manage by themselves, and it's been awhile. Mac is a prince, and the kids are great. I'm lucky Mac likes to cook. What would I do without him? I know I'm loved, and he knows he is loved, I think. The kids, well they aren't always so sure. Mac respects my need for freedom to move around, to search. He knows I'll come back more relaxed, ready to settle down again, to slow down. Nobody gets hurt. I don't think the kids suffer my being gone for short periods. They get to spend more time with their dad alone and collectively. It probably aids in developing some independence. I choose to think so.

There have been many studies of compatibility about families with multiple children compared to single child families as to which might be better. Which type of family functions more efficiently? Each has its advantages, I guess. Some say parents with a single child actually like (enjoy?) their kids more. Well, hey, where is all the rivalry, the cost, the mutual angst of a multiple? The joy can also be increased with all the additional possibilities.

Ziggy asks me when I'm going to retire. I don't call this working! This is living. Giving and receiving. What's better than spending your life traveling the highways and byways of life meeting people, bringing them things to treasure? They are willing to pay me for the service. I'm satisfying the needs of the shippers and the wants of the recipients together. The buyers and the sellers, they all have needs.

Well, I better move this along. I've taken too much time just enjoying myself.

I've got this longer trip to think about now. Among other things, I'll be hauling a heavy shipment of fine rugs from Dalton, Georgia to the west coast. Plan to head up to Sioux Falls, South Dakota. Make one delivery there. Then I can stop and visit Buster and Ziggy in Rapid City. I haven't seen them for ages. As long as I am in that area I should take the time to check out Mount Rushmore while I am there. I'll be heading up to Washington State and make a delivery in Spokane, then swing over to Seattle and pick up some partial less-than-full truck loads -LTFT 's- for my return trip.

These rugs are so heavy. What beautiful designs and colors. I think they used to be called "oriental rugs" or "The Tree of Life" pieces with fringe around the edges. All wool, no synthetics or man-made products. When did wall-to-wall carpeting come into style? And now, everyone wants wood floors again. Much of that wood product is coming from China and is of undesirable quality. There is no explanation for style, and each generation has to have its own fashion identity. But some styles, like these beautiful, and expensive rugs, never go out of style.

There must still be a lot of rich people in this country. People are willing to pay almost anything for what they consider beautiful. Beauty is in the eye of the beholder, we know that. I think it was Freud who said "A thing of beauty has no discernible use. Yet, without it life would be unbearable." That is so true! A thing of beauty is a joy forever.

I like to talk to myself out loud occasionally. It changes the air inside the cab. And my imagination is known to take off at such times. So, picture this; a person-sized capsule made of a soft, plastic material that a person would sit in. The size of an armed office chair in a weather controlled climate, air-circulating capsule, a soft plastic shell, that bumps would bounce off of, moving at a controllable speed, along designated areas, limited to certain walk-ways and drive ways. Let's call it a motorized BOBBLE. LET THE ENGINEERS AND DESIGNERS LOOSE on this one.

The BOBBLE could share the sidewalks with the dog walkers, neighborhood joggers, and skate-boarders. The BOBBLE would have to be plastic, bounce-able, able to right itself when tipped, like those old dolls that could right themselves when bumped. The kids would love to see old seniors tipping and rolling along on their neighborhood walkways.

The traffic on our highways is getting intolerable in some places. How can we accommodate the future traffic if it continues at this pace? The pile ups at the toll booths, the waits at the stop signs. People are spending half their lives in their cars. Why do we need a monster container capable of cruising at 70 MPH holding one 5 foot, 3 inch female, or a 300 pound guy who just wants to go and get a haircut?

What if we had special lanes for slower moving vehicles, and put the individual in a formed bubble, weather controlled, far from the madding crowd, getting to their destination in comfort and safety? It could be faster than sitting for hours on a blocked directional bridge. Get the designers busy, and put the bubbled lounge capsule back on the city streets, and in the neighborhoods. Send the speed highways around the cities on their outer rings. Driving lanes would have to be limited by mph speed limits. This road's vehicles cannot exceed such and such miles per hour. Of course, laws would be written and the change would not be done quickly, but if not now, when?

Which will come first? Individual vehicles carrying one person that fly above ground, like those hovering things, those drones, or a vehicle for a single occupant that maneuvers on the ground? It is sure to come eventually. If you can think it, then it can be done.

Time is like money. It is saved, invested, spent, and squandered. It is as valuable as gold. When you have a wish to do something special you dip into your bank of time and WHALLA!! it (time) is there. Why? Because it is a priority of yours. Your time is set on a priority scale. Your needs are weighed by you personally.

Consider moments like coins of small value. You can save them up by cutting out superfluous moves. Your habits, good or bad, will determine the amount of coins you will have collected. If you save moments by putting away things as you use them, you will have a collection of moments accumulated. Saving makes that account grow, with interest.

Big chunks of time are like valuable paper money. Save them for a big purpose. How do you use your discretionary time: hobbies, vacation, travel, golf? This is where your priorities depend on your spending habits. You have NEEDS. Some of your time will be spent on working, maybe a good portion. That is the spending of your time, the allotted minutes (hours?) you are using up. Study, learning, exploring, broadening your horizon is investing in the future. This account will be drawn on your whole lifetime. Sometime you will be making deposits in that account, and at other times withdrawals.

Your habits determine the speed at which you consume time. Habits that save time fill the account with spendable time. Your habit of preparing meals ahead, using the crock pot, laying out your work clothes for tomorrow, and multitasking are like coins, and other habits that use chunks of time are like big bills, paper money. Hopefully you will have accumulated a good amount of time.

Me, such a fountain of enlightenment. Saver of time! Well, I am satisfied by how my time is spent. Yes, even the traffic jams. When do you think this epistle was made? I get time with my family. I get time to travel and wonder at this great land! Time to reminisce about the past. I have time to be productive, giving a service that enriches me, and I don't mean the check I receive at the end of a delivery. A sense of contribution and accomplishment. I took the time to budget my time in my youth. I had good teachers. I made good habits. If you are lucky you may have had help and guidance along the way.

Have you ever known time to stand still? Or does time fly? How can it do both? Time is the only thing we share that is divided up evenly by regular increments and given to all of us. Your hour is exactly the same time span as mine. If you say you don't have time for something it means it is not a priority of yours. Your day has the same number of hours in it as mine. What you chose to do in those hours is your choice. Thank goodness for FREEDOM OF CHOICE.

The speed at which time seems to travel depends on what you are doing at the time. If you are waiting in the waiting room for your doctor's appointment the time crawls. If you have to get to the church with your groomsmen gifts before the service, and you haven't picked the gifts up from the engraver yet, time is your enemy and flying.

Personally, I believe people are like coins. They have two sides. One side is the face, or heads; the other side is the tails, or "bad" side. You could call them the right side and the wrong side. People can choose which side they want to use, what serves their needs. Their habits will determine which side they wish to favor, good or bad. The sides won't be used equally. Some may never use the bad side of their nature. It could be against their religion or training. It offends them to think they have the power to cause someone pain.

I understand that approximately 4% of our population is clinically psychopathic or sociopaths. They do not seem to have a conscience. They can cause pain in others without experiencing any concern. They are using the bad side of themselves, the bad side of the coin, with impunity. And they still have the good side which they find useful. They can be very charming. They can get sympathy, help from others, they can be loveable and loved dearly. An unsuspecting person can be fooled quite easily by their actions. Learn to watch for clues.

I remember the other night, Bud came to me with a sad look on his face. He's usually a happy go lucky guy so this was unusual for him. "I trusted her, Mom," he whimpered. "How could I be so stupid? It was going on right under my nose. What an idiot I've been! I can't trust my own judgment. I'm not a good judge of character, obviously. Am I so dumb?"

"Now, Buddy, don't be so hard on yourself," I said. "Trusting isn't all bad. Not everyone has your honesty standards. There are so many different kinds of people in this world with a wide range of standards. You'll learn that more as you get older. It doesn't hurt for you to learn it sooner rather than later."

"Yeah, well it cost me plenty," he said. "It hurts, Ma. It hurts really bad. It's going to hurt for the rest of my life. It's just not fair, not at all. I can't believe she could do that to me. I was so good to her. Too good! I'll never be caught like that again. But how can I be sure? I didn't see this coming. I can't trust my own judgment. I can't tell good people from bad."

"Well," I countered. "There are a lot of bad people in this world. Don't ever forget that. You will have to be more careful, and you have learned something that cost you in pain and money. You will survive, but you'll carry some lifelong scars. I'm very sorry."

Traffic is starting to move again. They finally got the road cleared of debris.

I think of life as traveling on a highway of life. Traveling offers you the opportunity to discover your gifts, talents and interests and how to put them to good use. What makes you feel alive? What makes you happy? What fills your creative need? The highway will offer you the opportunity to feel alive, to make you happy, and allow you to be creative and productive. Isn't that what life is all about? Make use of your senses. Feel it. All of it. Bless your senses. Activate all of them: sight, sound, smell, touch and taste.

You are experiencing the joys and sensations of being alive. THE TRIP'S THE THING. Don't give your destination your attention. You don't know what or where your destination is. By the time you have reached your destination your journey is over!!!

I always enjoy the planning phase in my trucking business. Plans are always challenging, and each planned trip is different. Variety is the spice of life. Life would be dull without it.

As you travel on the highway of life you will have to make plans, lots of them. Planning a trip is like a puzzle with creative thinking. It is challenging, fun, giving you a sense of accomplishment and great satisfaction. You might change the plan or abandon it. That is okay. It's still a plan. The execution of it is a whole different matter.

You have to LIKE THE PLAN. It must please you or solve some problem. It should have a goal, something that the plan can accomplish. It might ease your life, perhaps, or just get you from here to there. There are so many different sizes of plans. Some are for a day, a month, a life-time. Are you planning to build a piece of furniture or a trip to Europe? They all require planning. You may find out you're good at making plans and enjoy doing it.

Plans should be flexible, subject to change, even sudden change. You will be learning as you go along. Plans are not written in stone, maybe chalk or pencil. They belong to you so you have the freedom to adjust them as you go along. You might hit a BIG road block: a job loss, an unplanned pregnancy, a change in marital status, something that shatters your future plans. Now, what do you do? Your plans that were so well laid out are splattered all over the highway!!! Your plans have to be picked up, reworked, put back in order. NOW! IF WE COULD ONLY CHANGE THE PAST.

When you are traveling on this highway of life and your plans get changed, the first thing you do is slow down. You don't stop suddenly on any highway. You have to adjust your speed. You have to shift gears. Down shift, proceed slowly over the patchy stretch where all your careful plans are now strewn.

Are you a good driver, a careful driver? Then you must trust your good judgment in making different plans. Take the time to think about your alternatives. That doesn't mean you can't involve someone else in making or working with you on your change of plans. Maybe someone older, wiser, more experienced with the subject at hand. If you might benefit from help, don't hesitate to ask. People love to help and give advice. Makes them feel necessary, useful. Give them the opportunity to deliver the products which they carry with them. They may have just the expertise you need. Just don't make a decision in a hurry before giving thought and acceptance of a new version of your plan.

Remember, you have a history of good judgment. Trust it. When you arrive at the point of returning to your forward travel, your judgment will still be in working order. Trust yourself. Hopefully you have a history of good habits.

You will get to the place where you reach the mended patch and keep going. You've survived and maybe even prospered from the experience. It will have been an aging experience, and a learning one. Maybe costly, painful. Somehow you managed to make a correction. That's over now. Look ahead again. Keep on keepin' on.

HOLY COW! What is that black sedan up to? Yikes, a car full of teenagers. What is he going to do? I saw them parked in the lot at Duffy's awhile back.

Stupid kids. Not even legal. Too much free time. That speed means trouble. Sure, pass me, you idiot. GO, GO you son-of-a..... I don't want to see you in a pile all over the side of the road. You and your friends.

DAMN IT!!! No, no, oh no, not another. Sheriff, Mattie Wyfield here. Auto accident just west of Pine Grove on highway 15, 7 miles west of Duffy's, single vehicle accident, multiple casualties. Yeah. Car full of kids, been drinking. Good luck. Out. How many families will be crushed from this? Lives ended so fast. Damn the liquor. Would my kids do that? How can I prevent it?

The other night Jay was mad at me. He was yelling, swinging his arms about.

"That's not fair, Mom" Jay yelled at me. "Why do I have to pay rent to you and Dad just because I got a job now? No, I don't want to go to college. I'd rather take some vocational courses. You know, I tried to get a student loan benefit but you and Dad make too much money. That's not my fault. You are sending both Bud and Julie to college when they are ready, and you will be paying their room and board and tuition. What does that say about how you feel about me? Are they so much more important than me? Who is your favorite? It sure enough isn't me."

What can I say to that? "Oh, honey," I responded, "that doesn't mean we think less of you. You must know that, believe me. You have talents that the rest of us don't have. As soon as Julie and Bud get established in paying jobs, they, too, will be paying rent to us. If they make a higher salary they may have to pay a higher rent. We hoped you would find something you like that wasn't too labor intensive. Hard, physical work often has a shorter life span when you can work. We would like to see you get into something that taxed your brains rather than your brawn. We thought we could protect you. There are so many possibilities out there for you. You are a super smart guy as well as being so good looking. We don't have any favorites, you know better than that. It's like asking you which is your favorite finger."

"Truthfully," I added, "Dad wants you kids to have advantages that he didn't have. He thought college might give you more choices. But if what you want is not on the university campus there is no reason for you to go there. Just between you and me, Dad tried out the college gig and found it wasn't what he wanted, either."

"I don't care. And you can forget about your stupid fingers," he hollered. "You still expect me to pay you rent for my room and board. So just butt out, okay? I don't need your protection. Leave me alone. You won't be seeing me around here much, for sure. I got friends, you know. Just thanks for nothin'." He yanked his jacket off the hook and slammed the door behind him.

Heard the strangest thing today. A fisherman was walking along the shore of a river in Utah. He came upon an auto lying upside down under a bridge, windows all closed. He could see inside that the driver, a woman, was killed. It was later determined that the car sat along the side of the river 13 hours before the fisherman discovered it. It had a baby inside, a six month old little girl, still alive, now being treated at the hospital. Water was running through the car. It was cold. She's lucky to be alive. If it wasn't for that fisherman ...

I've got a stop coming up. Break time. Made good time today. Think I'll call home and find out how everyone is doing. Julie has a recital next week. I hope she has kept up her practice.

I'm so full of advice. You have to forgive me, but the experience that comes with the variety of traveling cross country delivering valuable products just blows the mind.

If you were to consider yourself a trucker, what products would you be transporting and delivering? The product that you will be delivering will affect the senses within you, most certainly. But also the senses of the recipient. The product that you will be carrying and delivering can't be packed into a container. If you are in the medical field, the product will be a sense of wellness. In the financial field, help and advice in the money and security field. You will be delivering peace of mind and a sense of security. These things are felt, not seen. But what precious products. Your remuneration, your payback, is the feeling of contributing, of personal satisfaction. The pay is good, too.

You won't need a truck to carry what you will be delivering. You will be carrying the product within YOU. What will you bring to those you meet? A happy face, a joke, an idea, an answer to a problem. After all, you will be educated or have a special interest in some field. Maybe you will have a job, a business, a talent. Your personality will be conveying feelings to others. (I hope you're not a grouch.) As long as you live, you will be sending out messages and leave impressions that will affect those you meet.

The big question is WHAT WILL YOU BRING TO THE PARTY? As you travel this mighty highway of life and participate fully, you will be delivering and receiving goods and services. You won't need a truck. Will you be delivering sociability, good humor? Everywhere you go you will be bringing your personal nature, your values, your preferences.

No two people are alike so each one adds to the stream of traffic on this highway of life. Each has unique gifts that they will be delivering. Some may make a big impression, while another might keep to the background. One makes a better party goer. Each individual will be made up of the results of his choices.

HABITS can be a good thing. A routine that you start can turn into a habit that you are hardly aware you're doing. So be careful of habits that you get started. You want good habits, not harmful ones. Samples, Good: exercise, cleanliness, food choices, things in moderation.

Bad: always late, sloppy, careless. I think you know by nature good from bad. The danger with habits is they can cut a deep grove. Deep habits can turn into addictions. If you practice moderation in all things, you will be fine.

As you travel the highway of life you will meet many people and have a lifetime of experiences. Hopefully, it will be a long life and a happy one. Like a highway, there will be hills and valleys, high times and low times. There will be accidents as well as smooth stretches, and some stormy weather. Your attitude will determine how your travels are judged by yourself.

You will not be able to level the bed of the highway, but you will be able to affect the perception of your lifetime of traveling on the highway. Your habit of good choices, positive attitude, time management, and a cheerful nature should assure you of a pleasant collection of memories as you continue to travel down memory lane. You want to be able to say "I had a good trip."

I personally wish you a long, joyful experience traveling on the highway of life.

BON ADVENTURE

Virginia Hult - March 2015

A PARADOX OF WISDOM

A lifetime of reading can be rewarding, beneficial, and stimulating. It can be broadening and enlightening. But it can, also, be dangerous. It can lead to bombastic pomposity, confusion and immobility. It is a prerequisite that an avid reader have an inquiring mind, with a desire to propagate his knowledge to the hungry masses in a magnanimous manner. But always keep in mind to keep it short and simple for the benefit of simple people.

A speaker needs a very extensive vocabulary in order to elucidate clearly his message to his audience. To do this demands an inquisitive nature and an expansive mind and body. This can best be achieved by reading a broad body of literature to expand your horizon and articulate your message.

A person's life is enhanced by a wide knowledge of indisputable information from which he can extrapolate his irrefutable conclusions. A library is a repository of inestimable knowledge that should be prevailed upon regularly to retrieve information for reference purposes and verification. Also, a Bookmobile or dictionary. A broad person should have a broad vocabulary to encompass the reprehensible information that rebounds in this world. An extensive vocabulary expands one's horizons and girth.

Your reading choices personifies your individual areas of expertise and allows you to circumvent the periphery with total confidence. Not to say that all of your reading should be circumspect, for one should indulge in some humor with a degree of propensity. To explore extensively only in one field of literature, i.e. history, biography, science or fiction, can lead to a very limited view of the world, or its surrounds. A narrow vision creates a confluence of conflicting compulsions which can, in time, affect a person's vision, especially if one has cataracts.

To elucidate further on the subject of the importance of reading, it is compulsory that a person have a questionable interest in many divergent fields. Broadening one's choices in literature, by its very nature, will make you a broader person. The mitigating effects of diversity are essential to a balanced life. The advantages of this are exclusivity and enlightenment to you and your audience as you divulge your expansive misinformation to the erudite masses that you commiserate with on a regular basis.

It is imperative that you disseminate your knowledge to your associates to impress them with your desire to share what you have learned from your own expansive reading. At the same time, one should eliminate any propensity for density. The propensity for verbosity can have a deleterious effect on the integration of your message. Brevity is essential for people with short attention spans or attention deficit disorders.

Sharing knowledge is a valuable gift, and it is a requisite for people of a generous nature and a teaching inclination to be diligent in this regard. To address an enlightened audience of your peers with your sagacious display of expanded knowledge and copious vocabulary will add to your stature as a conspicuous source of information, and bring you many friends and hangers-on.

Your conclusions may be counterproductive if not rendered in an understandable fashion. It is especially essential to be diligent in disseminating information of a serious nature in a deliberate manner. Your contribution to society is only limited by the extent of your social circle. The desire to enlighten the unwashed masses must be an ongoing compulsion if you are to have any influence in your sphere of influence.

Reading only for your own enlightenment is selfish and self-centered, and can lead to constriction of one's spirit. Unless your consumption is shared it becomes a burden of intangible weight which can restrict motion and activity. A lifetime spent reading, by its sedentary nature, leads to physical inactivity and even immobility if not interspersed by interchange with society. Paralysis can result from physical inactivity if not modulated with mindless exertion, such as jogging or tread-milling. The deleterious effect of consumption of unlimited information can only be mitigated by a deliberate system of delivery. Spread it around.

But there can be compensation, also in the form of expanding one's education to acquire fields of expertise resulting in advanced degrees, such as MD or PHD, with the corresponding expansion of remuneration.

The prevalence of stupidity is exemplified by the fame and celebrity of South Park and the Flintstones of this world. The popularity of ignorance is contagious and can spread and contaminate our vital organs. If the young of this world don't avail themselves of the wisdom and knowledge inherent in fine literature our culture is in danger of deterioration, or worse.

In conclusion, it is with trepidation my intention to elucidate the various aspects of extended participation in reading to the exclusion of other past-times. Its rewards are many, but its effects may be stupefying. It should be considered carefully to evaluate its value to an individual of sagacity.

Thank you for your indulgence.

V. Hult - 2009

THE NON-CAREGIVER

What would possess a man who has lived alone for 30 years choose to allow his mother and her dog to move into his house? Fortunately for me, this man is my son, Rex, who owned a home that had a complete apartment on the lower level that was empty. He was located in what I considered to be out in the country, whereas I had always lived in a city- like area with neighbors just over the back fence.

I was widowed and wanted to sell my big home. It was becoming too much of a maintenance problem for me to care to handle. After a few trial visits, staying over a weekend or holiday, I asked him what he thought of the idea of my moving into that downstairs apartment. His reply was: "Why not?"

I was pleasantly surprised. We expected it to be a win-win situation. He would benefit from the rent, and I would have a nice place to live. The sociability was a plus and my puppy was welcome. My son was definitely a homebody as was I, and he worked his business out of his home.

We started out shopping for groceries together, and I took it upon myself to plan and serve the evening meal. It turned out, however, I found myself eating the meals alone quite often, as it was not on his regular routine. We were clashing on the time schedule and each other's time routines. My efforts were going unappreciated, his freedom was being reduced. Words were flung. "I can not be a caregiver!!!" he said, smashing his fist on the counter. I saw red. I picked up the closest glass and flung it at the kitchen base cabinet where glass flew into a thousand pieces. I got up and walked away from the table, leaving the glass shards for him to pick up.

The boundaries were set. We each had our limits. "Oh, we don't want to make you mad," he said. Meal time was the determining factor. We tried pre-packaged meals, heated in the microwave oven. I lost interest in planning and serving the dinners. Sharing meal time but with separate menus eventually segued into Rex taking over the duties at meal time. I was most happy to give up that chore.

Having cooked for himself for 30 some years, this was not new to him. He took it upon himself to cook the meal, serve it up, and announce that dinner was ready. I never had it so good. I was certainly not used to being served by anyone. He kept wine in the refrigerator for me, served fresh chopped salads along with the meal. He began collecting recipes from the newspaper and experimented with new foods. He decided on the grocery selections and clipped coupons relating to his dinner choices. I couldn't rave more about the meals, the selection, and the variety. I reveled in my good fortune.

We slipped into a comfortable routine in our separate apartments. He gave me the opportunity to help him in his business by using my record keeping experience to record receipts coming in for his home business. This served to give him a paper trail on records he was keeping on the computer. Every morning he delivered the newspaper and his daily receipts to me after picking up his mail at the post office.

Most evenings Rex comes down after the news on TV and we discuss whatever. He snuggles with my puppy dog, Pepper, whom he feeds every day, takes to her groomer every other month, and accompanies her for her vet visits. His big dog, Winsor, had passed away just before we moved in.

Rex doesn't hesitate to give me his opinion: "You're not going to wear that! Those colors are so out of date. Your hair looks much better short." or "Oh, don't you look nice!" I had dressed up for a party at a girlfriend's house. He has a good style sense revealed in his collection of art works and pictures on his walls. I trust his judgment.

We both tend to be night people, staying up all hours at night, but not too active much before 10 o-clock in the mornings. He has an uncanny ability for timing considering he does not wear a watch. I am a stickler for being on time, always. I never want to be late. I am completely dependent on him to get me to an appointment on time and he amazes me with his punctuality. His business is run on an appointment basis so it is nothing new to him.

My puppy and I have been with him 10 years now. I pay for the groceries so we eat well. I make a list of my wants like cheese puffs and Nut Goodies for Rex to pick up, and he has his menu plans and coupons in hand. We have taken trips together by car and by plane. It's nice to have someone to hold on to walking thru the airport. We eat out a couple of times a month, or pick up submarines or pizza for variety. And so it goes…

I can't remember when we last had an argument! Nobody has mentioned anything about care-giving.

V. Hult - 2011

THE VIEW FROM MY WINDOW

My picture window sits over my living room couch like a huge painting hanging on the wall. It is a portrait of nature in its full beauty in every season of the year. There is a constantly changing picture bordered by a wooden window frame. Crank out windows are on either side of the picture window and serve to hold the blinds away from the picture perfect sight.

Every morning I gaze anew at this eastern view, a Christmas card scene in December, with snow frosting each bush and evergreen. A house high on a hill is visible now when the trees are bare. A snapshot in time. What a sight to watch the sun rise slowly, filling the skyline, majestically filling the room with light each day.

Some very artistic landscaper planted a garden in the front yard, along the driveway. A blend of bushes, spirea, barberry, pines, juniper, meugo, with a partially buried old wooden bucket spewing a carpet of creeping phlox, surround the bird bath and cherub holding a swan which I brought from my home. I had the statue patched and painted white last summer so now it glistens in the sunlight.

Last year my grown children took it upon themselves to improve my window view by taking a trip to the local nursery and stocked up on colorful perennials for my pleasure. They were on their hands and knees digging in the dirt, setting in asters, sedum, chrysanthemums, geraniums, and demanding that I determined the placement of each plant.

The garden is buried in snow at this time of year, but the view from my window is a constantly changing picture, offering anticipation of things to come.

Rebecca Park Trail, a fancy name for County Road 50, goes past my house so I watch whatever traffic there is on this 55 mile an hour stretch. Five, six o'clock in the morning is busy and around four in the afternoon, most likely workers on their way to work and returning home, but the rest of the day the road is relatively quiet. I have no trouble getting out of the driveway.

My puppy dog and I got a huge fright one dark night, in the pitch of blackness, when a big, white, furry face suddenly appeared in my window. I was dumb struck by this weird looking face, white hair standing straight up, two big black eyes, nose up against the glass, red tongue extended. Pepper went into attack mode, barking, growling, and clawing at the window glass. Fortunately, the stranger disappeared just as quickly as it appeared, dashing off in the night, the neighbor's white poodle puppy, just coming to visit.

Because my living room window faces a big, empty field, I haven't felt the need to draw the blinds closed. The closest neighbor is a far distance away, too far for us to see his comings and goings. A big weeping willow tree stands between us to help filter the view.

My window on the world is a constant source of interest, variety, and even surprises. It adds much pleasure to my life, and I am ever thankful for it.

V. Hult - 2011

AGING

I have nothing good to say about aging. You might expect an octogenarian to be an expert on the subject, so I should be an expert by now. But aging crept up on me while I was busy doing other things. I did notice I couldn't see so clearly. The world was gradually getting cloudier. People started talking lower. My television sound was getting weaker. Sidewalks were suffering apparently from more frost break ups, and steps were built with no uniform code. My car had grown wider over the years and turn signals were getting low on color. My Christmas mailing list had shrunk to almost nothing. Why isn't there a Tooth Fairy for seniors? I think my man-made teeth must belong to someone else!

Could my perception be the problem? I can't imagine. It has served me so well for so long. I had noticed that my pace was cut in half. My strength was reduced and my balance was uneven. My sensitivity is enhanced, a pebble in my shoe is unbearable. A strand of hair on my neck has to go. I bruise simply by leaning the wrong way. I can't always do what I want to do! Wait now... When couldn't I do whatever I wanted to do? Physically I suddenly found myself restricted. Stretching and bending were limited by old bones and muscles. Time to adjust, to admit and accept, to acknowledge this is what is called "aging". Even if you stand still and don't move a muscle, time marches on and you will continue to age.

Prepare to live with limits and losses. Time to adjust and accommodate living with limited resources. Limits are new to you: strength, energy, ability. Sad, angry? You choose. Hopefully, if you're lucky, you haven't lost your patience, your sense of humor, curiosity or ambition, nor your financial resources.

Will you know or admit when you are impaired? You may have to give up your car keys. You may have to learn to be dependent on others. Will you be grateful to them?

> Be careful what you wish for
> when your vigor's in full sway,
> Long life has its pleasures,
> but there is a price to pay.

V. Hult - 2011

MY HOMETOWN

I was born and raised in Minneapolis, Minnesota. That's my hometown. Minneapolis is also the birth place of many famous companies. Some worldwide known names originating in Minneapolis are 3M, Minnesota Mining and Manufacturing, for Scotch Tape, Pillsbury Flour Mills and Betty Crocker, the Dayton Company for Target, and Honeywell for thermostats and space instruments.

The name "Minneapolis" comes from the Native American Indian word "mine" which means water, and the Greek word "polis" meaning city, thus: water city. Minneapolis has 22 lakes within its border and calls itself the City of Lakes. It was founded in 1849 and covers roughly 58 square miles. At one time it was known as the Flour Milling Capital of the World.

My neighborhood was located close to the southern-most city limits, at the end of a streetcar line, at 50th Street and Penn Avenue. The streetcar had to turn around at the corner as it was the end of the Oak & Harriet line to prepare it for the return trip, and the screech of metal on metal as it reversed its direction could set your teeth on edge.

My block was made up of duplexes and single family homes built in a row on 50 foot lots, with a mix of middle class professional, business owners and salaried workers, home-owners and renters, and lots of kids on the block.

At the corner of the block stood a row of stores: a drug store, a grocery store, a butcher shop, a bakery, a dime store and a hardware store. Upstairs of the drug store, Dr. Allis had his dental office. With the stores just around the corner, at the end of my block, at 10 years of age I was able to run to the bakery early in the morning to get "1/2 dozen day old sweet rolls, please." Another errand took me to the butcher's for "4 thin pork chops" for 26 cents. This was in the depression times of the 1930's.

With 2 pennies to spend, I monopolized the drug store owner's time while I agonized over the many choices of candy displayed behind the glass case. One day he came out of his store to inquire if I had a license to sell the Kool Aid I had set up with a stand on the sidewalk outside his door on the corner. The streetcar conductor and motorman made such good customers as well as the passengers getting off at the end of the line.

Most everything was within walking distance of my home. I walked home from school for lunch each day. It was a quick turn-around to cover the 8 blocks in short order and eat lunch which my mother had ready for me. I was employed to walk Johnnie Knauff to and from his kindergarten on my return trip, for which I was paid a quarter each week.

Beside my school, the church and a movie theater in walking distance (matinee's for a dime) we were just two blocks from Lake Harriet, a beautiful city lake nestled within the city limits. Penn Avenue swimming beach stood at the bottom of the hill with the swimming area roped off, but no life guards. However, that was no problem. Very few people used the lakes at the time during this period known as the Great Depression of the 1930's. So many people were unemployed, recreation was an unknown activity.

We kids found recreation playing hide and seek, or kick the can in the alley, or cops and robbers with rubber band/wood block guns, and climbing in some under-construction building in the block. There were enough grade school children within our 1 square block to make up a good size gang.

To me, Minneapolis was a great place as a hometown, big enough but not too big, with all the amenities I would ever need, and the University at the end of my streetcar route on Oak Street. Downtown shopping was "out of this world" glamorous with The Dayton Company on Nicollet Avenue and Elizabeth Quinlan right up the street. And Packard's Shoe Store. The Guthrie Theater was just becoming known. The park system was carefully planned by Theodore Wirth to preserve so much of the landscape in its natural state, giving the city so many parks for family use and enjoyment. And there was ample opportunities to find employment downtown or within the city limits, once the Second World War ended the depression.

What more could one want in a hometown? I can't imagine. The edge of Rockford was the farthest I ever got from Minneapolis. That suits me just fine.

V. Hult - 2011

MY HOBBY

What kind of hobby can be done from an easy chair? What can I do that will give the impression that I am busy for a long period of time sitting in a comfortable chair? I would want a hobby that is portable. Not anything that would isolate me from people. It should be socially acceptable so I might carry on an intelligent (well, reasonable) conversation at the same time that I am working at my hobby. It should be something that doesn't require too many tools, and not too expensive. The necessary materials must be readily available and reasonable in price, also.

A hobby should be gratifying, satisfying, rewarding, and relaxing. To complete a project of value gives a sense of accomplishment. A hobby should require some concentration, maybe a skill, and a challenge is good. Knitting is a popular hobby for many people because it fulfills all these requirements. It is an easy process to learn and so many willing teachers are available. There is no time limit, no pressure to complete a hobby. Its' purpose is to make good use of your leisure time. It is especially healthy for senior retirees who are apt to have too much free time on their hands.

Knitting is one of my favorite hobbies. There are only two stitches you have to learn to do, the knit and the purl stitch. You do have to learn how to begin: to cast on, and how to finish: to bind off. You have to learn to read a pattern with its universal terms and abbreviations. There are a few tools you will need: an assortment of different sized knitting needles, a blunt end sewing needle, a knitting counter with pegs, a stitch and row measuring gauge, and a folding free standing material carrier to hold your tools and the project.

A knitting project can take months to complete. That in itself is a plus. You begin in the planning stage, choosing a project and finding a pattern. Then you acquire the materials you will need, what kind of material you will use, what colors you will choose. That sends you out shopping. Your enthusiasm starts to build. A new project gives you something to look forward to, to get you out of bed in the morning.

You choose a pattern, the harder the better, complex but within your range of ability. It represents to you a time for quiet activity, to listen to music, time to daydream, time for meditation when you arrive at a period of routine straight knitting over a stretch of the pattern. But be prepared for times of complete concentration such as: cast on 92 stitches, start by estimating how much yarn you will use for that number of stitches. 90, 91, whoops, two short, ravel and start again. Did you get interrupted while counting? Well count again. Yes, you were right. Now, let's start with 1 inch of ribbing, so knit 1, purl 1, repeat to the end. This first row of cast on is hard to distinguish, did I knit 2 in sequence? Well, just count from the beginning so you are sure to come out even at the end of the row, you should end with a purl stitch. *See below for news flash.

The hobby of knitting will be labor intensive, but with rewards on completion, intervals of pleasure, and times of not so much. There is delayed gratification, anticipation of a glorious ending, but with uncertainty just below the surface. How is that possible? Possibility of error is huge. You decide to use a bigger needle than the pattern called for. So you want a little bigger product. I hope it works out okay. Like a mystery novel, you never know how it will turn out.

Sometimes when knitting, one can get into a rhythm that leads to a loss of attention. Then one goes onto auto-pilot working on a long stretch with muscle memory taking over. Maybe thinking, what should we have for dinner, when, whoa!!! Now look what you've done!! Oh, no. I've been purling when I was supposed to do the knit stitch. Now, I've got to undo those stitches on the right hand needle and transfer them very carefully back to the left hand needle. What were you thinking? Well, I admit I knit while watching TV.

Sweaters, hats, mittens, I've made them all. The pleasure is in the knitting of the article, the process itself. Finishing off a project must be a part of every knitted article. This can include pinning, steam pressing and sewing the seams together. While the knitting of a front, back and 2 sleeves of a sweater involve many hours of work, assembling the pieces is a different task, a necessary evil, requiring a different discipline not enjoyed by knitters, or, rather, I speak for myself. It is the end of the project, aren't you happy to be done with it. No, not really. The finished product is incidental. Your friends and relatives may be inundated with your knitted items. You don't need to know how they use them. You have to go out and find a new project.

As long as my eyesight is good and my hands are steady I will continue enjoying the hobby of knitting. I look forward to always having a project on-going, and, usually a new one is in mind that encourages me to finish the current project. Obviously, I have a lot of free time.

*News flash

*Since this piece was written, I learned of a new way to determine where to set your starting loop which begins your first row. Simply wind your yarn around your knitting needle the number of times your pattern calls for you to cast on. Leave a short tail, 2 - 3 inches. It's as simple as that.

V. Hult - 2011

AN IDEAL JOB

Imagine, if you can, a job where you can work close to home, have all national holidays off with pay, spring vacations, Christmas and New Year holidays, summer months off (thou not paid), have your kids under the same roof? Why, the neighborhood school, no less.

For seven years I was the school secretary at Edina Highlands Elementary School. I answered the phone and greeted people in the front office. I worked with three different men principals during that time. There was, also, a Teachers' Clerk to assist the teachers with office needs. There was a fully staffed cafeteria crew and two men custodians. The classes ranged from Kindergarten to 6th grade.

The people were all pleasant, the hours were good, and the work was easy and enjoyable. The coffee was always available in the lounge for break time and lunch. A nurse was scheduled to be on duty certain days of the week at each school in the district, and was on call for any emergencies. I could settle a child down in the nurse's office. Calming a parent, however, was sometimes more of a chore. And don't interrupt an adult there to pick up a child from the nurse's office.

I had a key to the front door which I used to open the building a week before classes began. It was the time to set out supplies for the teachers and the schedules for the students. We had to know where each student was at any time of the day. This was before computers.

It was an added bonus having two of my children enrolled in the school where I was the secretary. Wait, now! Why has the playground monitor brought my son to the principal's office? Oh, this is embarrassing. There will be double jeopardy to pay when he gets home.

Getting to know the teachers over the years, my husband and I were fortunate to be able to host a couple of Christmas parties for the school staff at our home, which was in the neighborhood and large enough to seat 50-some people for dinner. Christmas music was provided by the music teacher playing on our electronic organ. My son's teacher remarked, "If this is how the secretary lives, I wonder how the custodian does."

I later went on to work at the high school office. The older students were fun to get to know. They would lean on my desk, to the principal's amazement, spending time just visiting. One habitually tardy boy liked the extra attention he got from me.

The principal tried to convince me to be his secretary, but that was a twelve month job which I didn't want. I liked my summers off, so I told him my husband didn't want me working in the summers. He asked if I would give in to my husband rather than to him, and I answered that after 25 years, I thought I should.

I continued in the school system until we eventually moved out of the district. By that time I was ready to retire, at least for a while. The next field I entered was as a Realtor. Now, that's a whole other story.

V. Hult - 2011

LETTERS TO ZIGGY & BUSTER

August 21, 2012

Dear Ziggy and Buster,

It is always so good to hear from you and to get your newest address. You folks are to be commended for your ability and fortitude to pick up and move as you have done.

Guess what!!! I, too, have moved. In the middle of January, Lisa and family came to Minnesota, and they convinced me to move to Missouri to live with them. Well, it didn't require much soul searching to convince me that that would be a very smart move. More creature comforts, more family activities, more hands-on help, what's to object?

I was with Rex for 10 years, and it was a very good time. He had said, from the start, "I'm not a caregiver." We both knew that, and for a time I did have a young woman come in to help once in a while. But I spent a lot of time by myself with Rex working out of his home, and he had to take me to doctor's appointments, etc.

Meanwhile, our precious Pepper was getting weaker,

mostly blind, her hind legs slipping out, losing weight, and with tremors, so we had to put her down. So Rex had to face losing, not only his roommate, but his beloved friend. Back to bachelor living again. He was not especially happy about it, but-----

I'm living the life of Reilly now, no doubt about it. To say I'm waited on hand and foot is no exaggeration. My library books are ordered on line from the local library and Dana picks them up on a regular basis. The meals that Em prepares every night are fantastic.

The kids all came here for my birthday. Paul, Shirl and Kyle flew in from Casper and Phoenix, and Rex drove down from Minnesota. They stayed for the best part of a week, Shirl got to shop in Springfield, Missouri; Paul was able to solve an electrical problem for the Fogles, increase water pressure in the shower for me; and Rex was busy looking at mini-storage places that were for sale. A good time was had by all.

Dana and her 5 year old son, Jacob, both started school. Jacob is in Kindergarten and Dana is back to classes for Occupational Therapy. Kyle had moved down to Phoenix to occupy one of two houses that Paul picked up, he is now entering his sophomore year in Business Finance at Arizona State University.

Well, I am happy I made the move. It was done in a rush, so I had Rex bringing some stuff down with him that we didn't take when Lisa drove me down here in my

Honda. Family pictures cover my bedroom walls. I sold my car so naturally I am driven wherever I want to go. You get the picture. Well, enough about me. I hope you two are thriving in your new location. Thanks for keeping in touch. Such good memories we have together!!!

Love,

Julia

August 19, 2013

Dear Ziggy and Buster,

Another birthday, another year! How can we accommodate so many? Who thought we would last this long? How many falls down the stairways, how many rides to the ER in the ambulances, how many bouts of pneumonia or liters of fluid drained are we allowed?

I always enjoy hearing from you at my birthday time. And I know we have to expect some bumps along the way. It is always good to hear such as Carol Mundt and her travels, selling Scandinavian objects and playing with an accordion club coming here to Branson!!! It is hard to compare with her.

But I am thriving here in Missouri (although they do have chiggers here!!!) not in Minnesota... Forgive me, but I am getting acquainted with a new computer that the kids presented me for my birthday and it is faster than I am used to. Must change some settings.

The kids all came again this year, Paul, Shirl & Kyle flew in from Wyoming, and Rex drove down (9 hours) from Rockford, MN. The Fogle house is big enough to comfortably hold us all. With Em in charge of the meals, we revel in fabulous menus with food in abundance.

I recognize the rainbow hues you mention and am sporting quite a collection from a recent trip to the hospital for a slight case of pneumonia, 4 days of pricks and stabs. Walking the halls (in two hospital gowns for decency) with a physical therapist recording my oxygen level (95) before they would let me go home.

I spend a lot of time reading. Found a new-to- me author, Swedish mystery writer that I enjoy. The first book of hers that I took out told of the Hult family as rogue faith healers! Camilla Lackberg, the author, is internationally well known.

I keep an ongoing knitting project at hand, been turning out scarves with a lace pattern I recently learned, that come in handy as gifts. Watch a share of TV and play computer games till my eyes get blurry. Did buy a piano off Craig's List (not the best tone) a Kimball, but it serves my abilities and Jacob has shown an interest in it so I got a beginner's book that we have started to look at.

The kid's visit gave me a chance to spend time with each of them individually during the quiet hours at night as I get up many times during the night and found one or another at the kitchen table relaxing.

Where ever do you find those animal pictures? That "real horse laugh" was just the type of thing I like for my bulletin board which I happened to ask Rex to bring down for me. I packed in such a hurry when I moved down to Missouri that I keep finding things I need here.

Thank you so much for keeping in touch, your card touched me deeply, no gift like friendship.   Love, Julia

August 16, 2014

Dear Ziggy and Buster,

Thank you for your annual greeting. Hope this finds you whole and happy. Me, not so much. In March I fell in my room at home and broke my right hip. Surgery put me back together again, thank goodness. After struggling with the walker, I have graduated to the cane, it's known as a Hurrycane. The hurry has not yet materialized. Had a couple months of physical therapy, do 5 laps around the living room before you sit down, do 2 sets of 10 Clam Shells each side (laying on your side, striking knees together), do 2 sets of 10 each Leg Lifts, practice going up and down the stair steps.... Continue this regimen when you get home. Sure.....!

Well, I'm getting along, moving a bit slower than before, but just lucky my new hip supports my weight without any pain. My special day was celebrated by just the five of us with a wonderful grilled salmon dinner by Em, and finished off with French Silk pie.

There was not the usual family gathering associated with August 15th this year as Paul's wife, Shirl, passed away at home on Sunday, August 3rd. Months of chemo and radiation treatments could not defeat the lung cancer. Paul accompanied her to hours of treatments. The funeral was in Casper on Friday, August 8th. Lisa and Rex both flew in for the funeral. I was able to watch the service via the web on Newcomer Funeral Home, Casper. So many people came out for the funeral as Shirl taught many years grades 2 and 4 there in Casper schools. Paul's office manager, Dean, wrote and presented the service, and Shirl's long time friend Phyllis helped feed the house guests at the reception after the service.

Kyle has returned to Phoenix now where he will be entering his senior year at the Arizona State University. Paul has carried on the long tradition of sending me flowers for my birthday, and this time they were silk flowers, so beautiful. He said he had to admit that all the other occasions I received flowers it was Shirl's doing. I said, "Oh, you must be kidding."

Movers are coming on Tuesday to move Dana's and Jacob's things out of the house here to their new apartment about 20 minutes away. What a change that will be!! Dana was fortunate to get a full time job at the new Mercy Rehab center here in Springfield. I will be curious to see how the Fogles adjust to the empty nest syndrome. Times they are a-changing....

Love,
Julia

NEW DAY DAWNING

Sunrise, bold and majestic!
God's promise kept, again.
A new beginning, another chance
To make a difference,
Create something,
Or even receive a gift.

A short hospital visit.
Some stranger's blood.
Strength and ambition returns.
A desire to wash windows,
Pick beans from the garden.
The future exists for you.

How long is the day?
Take it and run.
Enjoy the warmth of the sun.
As sure as the dawn,
Sunset will come.
God's pattern is constant and true.

V. Hult - July 2003

THE PHOTOGRAPH

A picture in hand is a ticket to travel,
not leaving your easy chair.
It projects on your mind a rolling screen,
past events come tumbling through,
To capture a moment, to treasure forever
the beauty, the joy, the life!

Some photos came in the mail today
that swept me back in time.
The Cap and Gown bear witness to goals
achieved o'er a period of years.
They record an event of tremendous content,
an achievement of struggle hard spent.

The family gathered to honor the feat,
and added its voice to the cheers.
Oh yes, we cheered when our own crossed the stage.
Shared success is ever so sweet.

We stood on the steps on a cold winter morn,
The doors of the building were locked.
The crowd milled about, waiting to start,
In pleasure, excitement and joy,
The close of one chapter, an end, to be sure,
but yet a beginning, as well.
What a story one photo can tell.

V. Hult - 2010

WHERE WERE YOU WHEN...?

Dec. 7th, 1941 is a date, as President Roosevelt said, "that will live in infamy." Japan attacked the American Naval Base at Pearl Harbor, sinking ships, killing scores of sailors, strafing cars driving on the streets. What were the Japanese thinking? The U.S. was fighting a war, the 2nd World War, in Europe. Japan thought we couldn't fight two wars at once.

Exactly 70 years ago, and yet I can vividly recall what I was doing when the news was broadcast on the radio. There was no TV in homes then! It was a Sunday afternoon. My parents were preparing to entertain their card club in our home. I don't remember where we lived at the time. They would be serving some coffee and a dessert which involved a rich, gooey chocolate concoction that set my teeth on edge. We were busy setting up tables and chairs in the living room. I remember arranging the tables with table clothes and setting the chairs. Suddenly an announcement came on the radio. Japan had bombed Pearl Harbor.

Our world was changed forever by that day. This event turned history on its ear! Things would never be the same. We did fight two wars at once. All the young men were drafted into service. There was gas rationing, and food shortages, coffee and sugar were scarce. My mother told of her standing in line for the longest time and when she got to the beginning of the line she found out it was for cigarettes, and she didn't smoke.

The United States dropped a single atomic bomb on Hiroshima on August 6, 1945, Japan surrendered. Japan was put under the control of General MacArthur for reconstruction after so much of Japan was destroyed.

Seventy years have passed, and I can still remember setting a table, such a mundane activity. I don't remember if cards were played that night. I don't remember what house I was living in then. This shows how life can change in an instant. Just a snapshot in time, setting a table, a simple task never to be forgotten.

V. Hult - 2012

MY ANCESTORS

My mother's name was Anne Augusta Eugenia Hellgren. She was born in 1891, January 7th, in Algetsboda, Sweden. She came to America around 1909 or 1910, probably when she was 18 years old. I am not sure of these dates. She came to New York after arriving at Ellis Island by boat. I think she traveled with a friend by the name of Anna Carlson who eventually had two sons named Homer and Virgil.

She traveled by train to Sturgeon Lake, in Minnesota, where she had some cousins. That may have been the family of Carl Lundell, I'm not sure. They helped her to learn the English language and she was enrolled for a time in the local school, where she was the oldest girl in 4th grade.

She also had an aunt living in Frederic, Wisconsin, and relatives living in Princeton, Minnesota. Her auntie in Frederic was Mrs. Thure Johnson, who had two daughters, Ruth Johnson, who worked in the bank in Frederic, and Anne Sommers, married to Reverend Sommers, who had a daughter Eugenia Sommers Kronour who now lives in Kentwood, Michigan. She has done extensive ancestral studies and is a good source of family history.

My father, Frans Arvid Lundberg, was born June, 1892, in Piteo, Sweden. He came to America and went thru Ellis Island sometime around 1910, I think. He left Sweden to avoid going into the Swedish Army. He was the youngest of 11 children, and his mother died when he was about 5 years old. He has a niece living in Piteo by the name of Jenny Persson, whose address is Hamngatan 59, B4, S-94162, Piteo, Sweden.

He spent some time as a lumber jack working in Northern Minnesota, and he also spent some time in Oregon. I believe my parents met in Minneapolis where many Swedes belonged to a group called the Good Templar's Lodge. It was a social club where immigrants could meet.

Anne Hellgren worked for a furrier in Minneapolis, Rockler Furs, sewing skins together and sometimes was asked to model fur coats for customers. She also worked for a time at Munsingwear, sewing piece work. Arvid was at one time a streetcar motorman and was paid $2.00 a day. He ended up working for Northland Creamery for 30 years, as the pasteurizer of the milk, controlling the machines that pasteurized the milk. He worked six days a week, and had every Thursday off. He finally retired at the age of 56, and retired to live in Florida where he loved the weather and the outdoors. They celebrated their 55th Wedding Anniversary in St. Petersburg,

Florida. They, also, had a number of different lake cottages in Minnesota because they both liked the outdoors and loved to fish. So they would spend the summers in Northern Minnesota and the winters in Florida.

Anna was a stay-at-home mom, but she had a great interest in houses which caused them to own many different homes, as well as rental property. She liked to fix them up and then sell them. This caused them to move many times and Virginia attended a number of different schools when growing up.

Their friends called them Anna and Arvid Lundberg. They had two daughters, Mildred Elvira, born February 27, 1917, and Edith Virginia, born August 15, 1926. Mildred married Willard A. Olson and they had three children: Dianne, John, and Elizabeth. Virginia married Theodore Hult and they had three children: Rex, Lisa, and Paul.

Virginia Lundberg Hult

A Poodle's Tale

A dog with an attitude speaks her mind.

Chapter 1 - MY STORY

My name is Pepper, and I'm two years old. I was only nine weeks old when Julia adopted me. I am 12 pounds of bubbling energy, famous for running figure eights around the house and yard. Miniature Poodle is a label I carry.

I was the "pick of the litter," much more lively than my brothers. And I am truly blessed with exceptional intelligence and good looks. My beauty has stopped people on the street to admire my curly black hair and ask permission to pet my fuzzy head. My personality is very outgoing, with bursts of enthusiasm that can knock a person over. I love people and other dogs. My sire is a Schnauzer-Poodle mix, my dam is a Poodle. That makes me a Schnoodle. Schnauzers are characterized as being self-assured, Poodles as clever. I am proud to be a Schnoodle.

The woman who owns me is an older, gray-haired person. That's Julia. She moves too slowly on our walks. I have so many things to sniff and investigate, and her slowness gives me a sharp pain in the neck.

The charms of femininity were stolen from me at an

early age by a veterinarian's sharp knife. The additional indignity was added of making me wear a white plastic cone on my head to prevent me from even the slightest satisfaction of biting my surgery stitches. Then, to add insult to injury, a white body suit denied me the comfort of scratching. Julia tried to appease me with offers of some Milk Bone treats [and I do love them] but I summarily refused them, as if I would forgive her for what she had done to me.

I attended and graduated from Good Doggie Manners I and II, and have diplomas to prove it. The second class was much harder, we had to perform a trick to graduate. I, of course, did my usual "sit and shake hands" to get a treat. I flunked "sit and stay" but that was because all the other dogs in the class kept distracting me.

When Julia sits down to read the paper or a book, it is an invitation for me to jump into her lap. I love to snuggle, and I never fail to reward her with a kiss to her face. TV- watching provides me another opportunity to cuddle. And, oh how I love to have my tummy rubbed. Whenever she is dressing, I'm there with my legs waving in the air, flat on my back, begging, please, please give me a rub with your bare feet.

I've trained Julia in a few ways. There is a brass bell hanging on the door knob that I ring when I want Julia to come and open the sliding-glass door so I can go out in the yard. I also ring it when I just want to see if she'll come. So far, she does. As for feeding, dog food, although it may be nutritionally balanced, is dull and tasteless. Julia has learned that I am much more willing to eat it if she serves the brown nuggets on a plate of her china. I like the white plate with blue flowers around the rim, or the bowl with a small pink rose on it. I think presentation is everything.

I feel I have certain responsibilities around the house. When someone rings the bell or comes to the door, I announce them loudly. I always let Julia know when the mailman is here. When someone parks in front of my house, I let them know this territory is already taken.

Julia kept me in a kennel crate at night for my first year, but now she lets me sleep with her at night. That is so much better, there was no down comforter in the crate, and no body to snuggle up to. I am on guard all night long, and I am a good watch dog. If there are any strange noises I give a warning growl, and no prowler would dare to come near, as I would jump all over him. That is another one of my jobs here.

When I was little, Julia would close me in the porch if she was gone from the house for short errands. I showed my disgust by chewing on the wood arm of one of the wing back chairs. I also managed to chew a hole in the seat cushion of the matching chair. She didn't like that, and went to a lot of trouble sanding and re-varnishing that wooden arm on the chair. They were so old, I don't know why she bothered. Now that I am older and more responsible, she leaves me to have the run of the house, except her bedroom where the lavender velvet pillow and her slippers are kept.

Ron, Julia's son, claims that I was "spooked by a paper bag." I was not "spooked by a paper bag." If an alien object suddenly appeared in his front yard, he would expect me to sound an alarm. When it did not react to my warning barks, I was suspicious. As caution is the better part of valor, I approached it very slowly. It did not move, and it was taller than me. The paper bag had not been in the garden before. It did not belong there. A paper bag is not designed to hold weeds from a flower garden. Anything new, or strange, or out of place gets my attention. I am very observing, and people should appreciate my vigilance.

I love Julia so much. She is the most wonderful person I have ever known. Although she bought me, she knows I am not her slave. In fact, she treats me as the royalty that I am. I am a true princess, and she treats me accordingly. I am trimmed on a regular basis, and come home with bows in my hair. She combs the long hair of my ears to give me a glamorous look. She keeps the rest of my curly hair trimmed quite short. Julia is so good to me. Her fingers are moving constantly, scratching under my long ears, around the collar on my neck, petting the top of my head. She just can't keep her hands off of me. I love it.

Chapter 2 - COUNTRY LIVING

We have moved to the country! We are now living in Ron's house with his four acres of land and many outbuildings. There are farm fields across the road. The streets are gravel roads, and we have no close neighbors. There is an old barn on the lot with holes in the floor and stuff stored all over the place. The floor boards are broken and you can see right down to the cow barn below.

His house is nice, and we (that is Julia and I) have a pretty apartment downstairs. Of course, we go upstairs whenever we like and spend just as much time upstairs with Ron. They always eat together and they feed me in Ron's kitchen. Julia does most of the cooking and Ron does the cleanup. Ron gives me food from the table if I dance around for him but Julia doesn't.

Now that I have so many acres to run in, I really enjoy the freedom and wide open spaces. But one Saturday when they were both ignoring me, I took off running across the road. Cars were coming but I saw them and they slowed to a stop and pulled over to the side of the road. But Julia got so excited, she started yelling at me and started running after me. No way could she catch me at her speed. Then she yelled for Ron to come and catch me. He had to drive his truck to catch me. I was in a farmer's yard by that time and when Ron offered me a ride, I gladly accepted the offer. Now, for some unknown reason, they hook me up to a long rope and chain whenever I want to go out in the yard.

What happened? The world turned white overnight. Julia let me out the backdoor and everything is white and wet. I don't like this stuff. It is wet and sticky and cold. It makes me wet and cold and it sticks in my fur. It sticks in my paws, and it is cold and wet. I don't like this stuff and hope it goes away right away. We never had this stuff in the city. Is this because we are out in the country where there are farms across the road that they have this white stuff? The yard is all white. The trees are covered with white stuff and white stuff is falling from the sky. What is going on?

Julia lets me out every night before we go to bed. When I come back in, my feet are wet and my legs are covered with snow and ice. She doesn't want me in bed with her with my wet, snowy feet so she has tried to wipe me off with a towel and used a brush with sharp metal teeth to get the ice chunks off my legs. That just wasn't working well enough, so the next night she decided to put some nylon socks on me that she could just pull off with the snow clinging to them. They felt strange on my feet and they looked ridiculous. The back pair did not even match the front black ones. But, it was dark outside, so I did walk out into the snow in the yard. I was out a long time, much longer than normally. Julia got worried. She is a worrier. So she came out to look for me. I finally came in, but without the socks. They won't find those socks until next spring.

Chapter 3 - A TRIP TO WYOMING

Julia spanked me. She yelled at me. I think she swore. I got up during the night. She was sound asleep. I needed to go out. There is no bell on the door in the kitchen. Should I have disturbed her? Well, I had to go, so I went pooh on the rug by the door. When she saw that in the morning, she got so mad. Boy, was she mad! What do people think? She has finally learned to let me out during the middle of the night so there has been no problem with her since that night.

We took a trip for Christmas, drove all the way out to Wyoming. I had the whole back seat of the car to myself. Two days' of riding, we stopped at the rest stops in South Dakota, where it was really cold with the wind blowing like mad. We went to visit Julia's other son, Paul, and his family. They have a new puppy they are so excited about. He is black and white, and what a pain. His nose is pushed in, and his eyes bug out. He was all over me, he nipped at my ears, and he chased me all around the house. The only way I could get away from him was to jump up on a couch or up into someone's lap. He was too little to jump that high, although by the time we left, he had learned to jump up onto the couch. He wasn't house broken yet, and half the time I was blamed for his accidents. What an insult!

On the way home, I had to share the back seat of the car with a huge black plastic bag of tumbleweed. A friend of Ron's asked him to collect and bring back dry tumbleweed that he uses to create small trees for his model railroad systems. There is tumbleweed blowing all over Wyoming, and it collects in piles against Paul's fences. They had no trouble gathering a full bag in a short time. When we got home, Ron's friend looked at the bag full and said it was the wrong kind. When is tumbleweed not tumbleweed?

Coming home from Wyoming, we made it to Chamberlain, South Dakota, on the first night out. Ron and Julia started looking for a motel for the night. Julia wanted to stay in a motel that opened onto the parking lot to make it easier unloading whatever they needed from the car. They passed up plenty of motels with very few cars in their lots, but she wanted to go to one she was familiar with in downtown Chamberlain.

When we reached Chamberlain, she went in and told the clerk she wanted a smoking room, two beds, and she had a small poodle. The woman told her that her smoking rooms were all full, but the dog was no problem. So Julia said they would take a non-smoking room then if there was no other choice. "No," the woman said, "I can't rent a non-smoking room to smokers because they will smoke anyway." So Julia says

"You mean my dog is acceptable to you but we are not?" The woman apologized but said that was basically correct.

They drove off to find another motel. Not a word was spoken but I could hardly keep from laughing. They ended up at a Holiday Inn, walking through the lobby and down a long hall, with me on a leash. I held my head high, full of pride. I guess that showed them. I am more acceptable than they are.

Chapter 4 - BODY LANGUAGE

The other day I heard Ron ask Julia, "How did this piece of fudge come to be on the living room rug?" Julia said, "Why, I have no idea. The candy box has been on the kitchen counter all the time. Pepper can't get up on the counter, can she?" Ron said, "No, I don't think so. That is too high for her to jump." "Has it been chewed on?" Julia asked. "No," Ron replied. "It doesn't look like it." A few days later, Julia came into the dining room and found me sitting on the high stool next to the kitchen counter. She told me to get down. I don't think she suspects a thing. Anyway, I found out I don't like chocolate fudge.

I don't speak words like people do, but I do know what they are saying. Words like "down" or "come" or "go for a ride" I understand and can choose to react or not. I am more influenced by a person's tone. Are they happy, serious, angry? You can always tell by how they sound. But I think Julia lied to me the other morning. Sunday morning we slept late and the sun was shining so bright. I let Julia know that I wanted to go outside. She let me out the door, but because she is so stiff with arthritis in the morning I got away from her before she could hook me up. I started trotting off for a good run. She called to me but I just kept going. So she called, "Want to go for a ride?" I came running in right away. Then it sounded like she said something about "well, not now."

I speak with body language. And that is always honest. My ears perk up when I am listening with interest. My tail wags when I see someone I like. You can tell I am happy. I jump for joy when Julia or Ron comes home after being gone for a while. Ron went out the other evening to visit friends, and I kept watching for him at the window for the longest time. Yes, sometimes I get anxious.

Eye contact is so important in speaking body language. I look directly at someone when they are speaking. Sitting and staring is very effective, especially when they are eating. The non-blinking stare works well when Ron or Julia is eating ice cream. They usually leave me some ice cream in the bottom of the bowl rather than finish it themselves. Silence can be a very positive tool in language. Sometimes a sharp bark and a quick paw to their legs are needed when they are deliberately ignoring me. If nothing else works, I just jump into a lap and settle in.

You know, God didn't create me to live alone. I can't feed myself. Other animals can forage for food, or hunt for smaller beings. I can't catch mice or eat bugs. Dogs can only survive if they are part of a pack or have a caretaker. I can't live outside in heat or cold without some kind of shelter. Some animals burrow underground or can live in a hollow log. I know I'm very lucky to have soft cushions to sleep on inside a warm house, and food offered to me twice a day. What can I give in exchange? I give them entertainment. But, mostly, all I have to give is love. Maybe, that is enough.

Chapter 5 - JULIA'S SECRET

I was lying on the cushion at the end of the couch listening to Julia talking with her niece the other day. "You know, Julia," her niece was saying, "You had such a good marriage. You were married for over 50 years. People have a hard time doing that now days. You must have a secret to your success."

Julia chuckled. "Well," she said, "if women treated their mates the way they treat their pets, they wouldn't have so many problems." I perked up my ears, wondering what she was talking about.

"Of course," she continued, "the breed you choose is most important. Do you want a hunter, a sports breed or a show dog? Should he be a pedigree with papers or a mixed breed? Breeding gives you clues as to how they will mature. And looks are very important. Do they meet your criteria of 'handsome' or 'attractive'? Are they lively and sociable? Have they been hurt or abused by former owners?"

"Once you have made your choice," she continued,

"you have to love them and pet them, scratch their backs and rub their tummies. You should play with them. You need to tell them how beautiful they are and how smart they are. You have to feed them and groom them. You show them tricks and rave how clever they are. You have to take them in for check-ups and to get their shots. You go out for walks with them every day. They must feel free and confident of your trust. And when you whistle for them to come in, you call and say 'I have a treat for you'."

Well, I guess that's all true, but then, why does Julia hook me up to a chain when she lets me out in the yard? She doesn't trust me. Apparently, Julia's husband never strayed from his yard or ran after cars.

This morning I barked in Julia's face to wake her up. It was Sunday morning and it must have been ten o'clock. We had slept long enough. I wanted to get up and play, so I jumped on her stomach. That got her up. I always sleep with her now. I curl up and lean against her back. She usually moves away to give me more room, but I just get up and curl up against her back again. I just like that contact. When she gets out of bed, I move over onto her pillow and sleep awhile longer.

I still get up during the night, usually around 1:30 or 2 o'clock, to go outside. Now, in order to wake her up, I find her face in the dark and I give her a soft kiss on the cheek. That wakes her up in good humor and she says, "Oh, do you want to go out?" I stay out just a few minutes, and I am able to push the outside door and the kitchen door open to get back in. Then Julia gets up, saying, "Pepper, you didn't close the doors and shut off the outside light." Sometimes I'm back in bed before she is.

Chapter 6 - FAMILY REUNION

Julia's family got together for a family reunion at Ron's place the last week in July. Her younger son drove up with his family from Wyoming in their big motor home. Wouldn't you know it, they brought their dog! A pushed-in-face Boston Terrier, black with some white markings. Julia's daughter and her family drove up from Tennessee. Sure enough, out of the car jumps Mickey, an old black Schnauzer with thinning black and gray hair and a skin condition. They're staying for a week!

The folks were so excited and happy to see each other, it had been a long time since they had been together. I can remember seeing the Schnauzer when I was just a puppy, and I could easily take him down, get him on his back, and nip his ears. Now that Mickey, and I, were older we respected each other. Besides, he had a delicate stomach and was inclined to throw up.

The Boston Terrier, Harley, (Julia kept calling him Rambo) would not leave me alone. He chased me all over the house. I would hide under the coffee table but he would find me there and nip at me. I jumped onto any available lap, but he just kept coming at me. The folks laughed and said he was just a puppy, as if that was some excuse.

Harley ruined Ockie, my toy octopus!!! He bit him in the head and chewed out his brain, his voice, his squeak box. It was my favorite toy, given to me by my breeder when Julia adopted me. I used to grab on to one of its six legs and fling the octopus across the room. I could shake the daylights out of him and he never complained. Now he has a hole in his purple head. He is brain dead. Julia says she can stitch up the head. What good is a brain dead octopus?

One day, the young folks had places to go, visiting friends or seeing the Mall of America. So Julia was left alone with us dogs. She decided to get us out in the backyard. My rope and chain were fastened to the bottom rail of the porch stairs. She hooked me up there. Harley's rope was wound around the big maple tree. And the rope for Mickey was connected to the flag pole. Julia had all she could do to get all three of us hooked up at once. Naturally, the ropes got tangled up as we ran around. Harley was standing on my rope so I couldn't even move. Mickey was barking up a storm.

Julia decided to separate us and moved Mickey's line to the bird house pole. That gave him a much bigger range to run. Next thing I knew he was up on the deck. I barked at him in no uncertain terms, "Get off my porch."

He barked back, "Mind your own business!"

What was he doing up on my porch? I was furious. "Get down off that deck," I barked. Julia decided to let Mickey into the house. If he could be in the house, then I should be able to be inside, too. "Let me in," I barked. So Julia unhooked me and let me go inside.

That left Harley alone chained up in the yard. "Don't leave me here by myself," he barked. He carried on like some cry baby, howling and barking and whining.

Well, I got up in the living room window and barked for him to "Shut up!" Why Mickey kept up his barking, I don't know, but Julia finally closed him in the back bedroom. Even that didn't quiet him down.

Julia finally decided to bring Harley inside, too. That was all that was needed. We were happy to be together and everyone settled down very nicely.

One day Julia's son from Wyoming came in wearing brand new sneakers. They were black with white markings, and looked to me like two big dogs. I ran and hid in the corner behind the big chair. He tried to approach me. We had been friendly before and he couldn't understand why I wouldn't come near him. No way was I going to be in the same room with those big puppies.

Harley had a habit of hiding his treats. Did he think he was a squirrel? The folks brought home three huge bones from a dinner they had after a night out at a restaurant. Harley immediately took his bone and hid it under the motor home. I enjoyed mine out on the deck, cleaning off all bits of meat I could find. Mickey couldn't have any of the bones because of his delicate stomach, so I suspect Harley stole his bone, which never showed up again. And the clean bone that I finished off also disappeared. Julia later found a partially chewed chew stick in her bedroom closet hidden among her shoes.

The week finally came to an end and the folks all packed up to go home. They all expressed their joy at the good times they had. They had enjoyed great meals, cook-outs, card games, lots of talk, even fireworks, thanks to Julia's grandson. They were celebrating Julia's birthday. The whole week was one big party. They were sorry to see it come to an end. But not me.

I have the house to myself now. What a relief! I can sleep in peace again. But it is quiet, so quiet, so quiet...

Chapter 7 - PEOPLE TRAINING

People are ideal subjects for training. They have the ability and the capacity to satisfy your every need. They can give you housing, food and comfort. It is well worth your time and effort to adapt them to your desired results. With patience and persistence they learn quickly. They seem eager to please.

I have been very successful in training Julia and Ron, and they have been willing participants in these efforts. Most dog owners are dog lovers and should respond in like manner if given the opportunity. This is a win-win situation that gives satisfaction to both parties. I, Pepper, win; Ron and Julia benefit.

I am surprised by how quickly people can be trained. For instance, I have taught Julia and Ron to respond to a bell. I ring a bell; they come running. No matter where they are, what room in the house, whatever they are doing, if I ring that bell, one of them will come to me. I've heard Julia call out, "Ron, was that Pepper ringing her bell?" And Ron will answer, "Yes, I'll get it."

The bell is tied to the door knob of the sliding door

that leads to the deck and the backyard. Whenever I want to go out, I just ring that bell. It works every time. They are quick to respond. I even rang it once when I didn't want to go out, just as a test. Julia came immediately. She passed the test. I haven't tried that since.

You teach people how to treat you. To get respect, you must demand respect. I have taught them my food preferences. I don't like food in that blue rubbery dog dish. I prefer to eat off of the same dishes that people eat on. People's plates are cleaner looking, more appetizing and attractive. I think presentation is everything. The dinner plates are bigger, and my ears don't get in my way like they do in that dog bowl with the high sides. And the plates often have bits of meat left on them, especially Julia's plate. Ron leaves steak sauce which wrinkles my nose and always gives me a face that they laugh at.

Julia adds dog food to the plate and mixes it with the leftovers, so sometimes I have spaghetti sauce or garlic sauce and pasta coating the dog food. I like left-over onions, or even salad dressing on the dog food. And I love desserts. Ron and Julia will leave a little ice cream for me in their bowls, because I sit and stare at them while they are eating. I clean those plates as well as any dishwasher.

I have found a way to get treats on demand. People cannot refuse me. I stand right in front of them and stare until I make eye contact. A statuary stance at their feet, with a direct eye-contact stare, will get them out of their chairs most of the time. If necessary, I sometimes have to resort to a low growl or sharp bark, but it moves them every time. They may not always be willing, they may respond reluctantly, but they do move. You have to be persistent and patient in training people. They like to please. Pleasing me makes them happy.

Independence is good, but dependence is better. Depending on a person makes them feel needed, important and gives them purpose. It makes them better people, more generous, more disciplined. The weak enslave the strong, but that makes the strong stronger!!!

There are times when Ron and Julia have been gone from home for hours at a time. They leave me alone in the house. I do not like being left alone. I am a social being who likes activity and personal interaction. When they return home I am in their face letting them know that they owe me some attention. I jump up on them, I run around them, I perch on top of the lounge chair wiggling and shaking. At that level they cannot ignore me. They feel guilty and make apologies and usually have some restaurant doggie bag or treat to give me. They have good intentions, but there are times when they are somewhat thoughtless.

The secret to training people is to show them you love them. I do that every day without a word being spoken. It is all done with body language and body contact. People need love. They have to see it and feel it. Julia and Ron know I love them. They see it in how I greet them whenever they have been gone for a while. They feel it when I lean into them sitting in a chair or in their beds. I squeeze in beside them when they are lounging in the recliners. I press against their backs in their beds. Contact is so important in body language.

Training without love is almost impossible. The desire to please the trainer is necessary to accomplish the end result of any learning experience. People will not perform for you if they don't care about your feelings. They have the choice to perform or not. So what makes them give you the desired result? They choose to please you because they love you! In return, you give them companionship, entertainment and love. The purpose of training is to shape behavior to fit your needs, and a trained person is a joy to live with.

Chapter 8 - THE BIRTHDAY PARTY

Julia had a birthday on the 15th of August this year, 2006. She was 80 years old, which I guess is supposed to be old for people. I'm seven years old this year and I'm feeling my age. I sleep most of the day, my hair is turning color, some gray, some brown, and I suffer from allergies and bladder stones. I don't know what Julia suffers from but she sleeps a lot, her hair is mousy colored, and she moves awfully slow.

Her kids came from out of town for this birthday, her daughter's family from Memphis, Tennessee, and her younger son's family from Casper, Wyoming. They flew in this time. Lisa and Dana and Em came the Saturday before the birthday; Paul, Shirl and Kyle missed their plane on Saturday (something about overload or weather conditions) so they got here the next day. They were all here at Ron's house by Sunday. I, Pepper, was not disappointed that the dogs, Toby, Ginger and Harley stayed home.

The weather was beautiful, sunny, blue skies, nice breeze, even Paul admitted Minnesota could be nice. Julia's nieces Dianne and Liz came for the party. Ron grilled brats and chicken out on the deck. I begged and whined for samples but hardly got any of the brats, and just a little chicken. Maybe some of the left-over brats. None of the potato salad, fruit salad, and certainly not a taste of the Key Lime Pie or Carrot Cake that had birthday candles on them.

Dianne brought a tiny flannel shirt for Dana's baby due in January so he can go fishing with Em in style. And there were a lot of gifts for Julia. Her kids gave her a new light fixture for her kitchen so she can see to do her jigsaw puzzles at night. Lisa decided the other light fixtures all needed washing. She managed to shut down all the power in the house and set Ron's hair on end when his computer and shop ovens went out. She made up for it later when she stepped down into the wash bucket and let out a yelp. Everybody else rolled in laughter.

Kyle found an old abandoned Honda motorcycle in Ron's barn that made his week. He and Paul spent the week cleaning, fixing and replacing parts for it and were surprised and delighted when they got it running. Kyle managed to put over 20 miles on the odometer riding around Ron's acreage, and can't wait to get the motorcycle shipped back to Wyoming. A 15- year-old's dream come true. He couldn't keep from smiling. Ron even found a helmet for him that had been left in one of his self-storage units.

The kids decided to have Julia's car detailed for her

birthday. The man detailing the car spent one whole day working on it and it was returned looking brand new. The interior was all shampooed, the windows all washed, the chrome polished, the body waxed, the tires shined. She hardly recognized her 11-year-old car when it was driven onto the driveway.

Shirl had a dream week of shopping the whole area. She took in the Arts and Craft show in Buffalo where they were staying at the motel. She got to Kohls in Maple Grove and up to the big outlet mall in Albertville. She had the whole family worried when she didn't get home 'til midnight from that mall. Seems she got lost leaving the mall and ended up in north Minneapolis when she called Ron to direct her out of that neighborhood. He told her to close her windows and lock her doors and find Olson Memorial Highway which would get her onto Highway 55 and back home. That tour of Minneapolis scared her plenty but did not squelch her love of shopping.

Julia got a lovely sterling silver necklace for her birthday with birthstones inset in the pendant. Liz identified and recorded the different stones for Julia's information: a peridot for Julia, pearl for Lisa, emerald for Ron, sapphire for Paul, turquoise for Dana, and ruby for Kyle.

All that week I was skittering around on the rug on my bottom and Lisa and Shirl decided that I had worms. What a disgusting thought! I wouldn't have worms.

Julia asked Ron to find a sample of "you know what" to bring for testing. Just imagine him searching over his 4 + acres for that. Well, I left what he needed on the rug by the sliding glass door because he didn't get up when I rang the bell at 4:00 A.M. I am very helpful.

They had to take the sample to the vet. Julia had to call Paul who was at the motel. Ron was in Wisconsin handling two rentals and a break-in at his storage facility. Julia's car couldn't be used as it was still wet inside from the detailing and the car mats lay in the driveway behind her car. The vet clinic was closing at noon because it was Saturday. Paul and Julia drove over to the clinic with the sample. The receptionist asked for the symptoms and suggested they bring me in to be seen. So they came back and picked me up. Well, it was determined that my anal glands were swollen and the clerk was able to treat the condition. No worms, but I'm still scratching all over from my allergies.

Ron managed to get some work out of Paul and Kyle while they were here. They spent a whole day in Cannon Falls at Ron's storage facility. Ron rented a bob cat and ordered 7 truck loads of gravel. He used Paul's expertize to run the bobcat while Kyle and Ron raked and shoveled, leveling and spreading the gravel around the different buildings. They came home late that night dirty and tired but very pleased with all they accomplished.

The week went fast. Everybody seemed to have a good time. I am now back on my regular schedule of eating and sleeping and Julia is doing the same. The kitchen is brighter. The car is cleaner. The refrigerator is full of leftover food, pop, and bottled water. Boy, some people sure know how to party!

ABOUT THE AUTHOR

Virginia Hult was born in Minneapolis, Minnesota and lived in and around Minneapolis for the first 84 years of her life. She then moved to Springfield, Missouri in 2012 and has been part of a 4 generation household living with her daughter, son-in-law, granddaughter and young great-grandson. She enjoys reading, writing, doing word puzzles, knitting, and playing the piano.

Virginia has said, "My trip on the highway is over. I have reached my destination and there is no other place on earth that I would rather be."